A Gift For

....
From

....
Date

....

Mark Gilroy

the
Simple Blessings
of *Christmas*

A Hope-Filled
Journey Through the
25 Days of Advent

Contents

Foreword

My favorite time of year is Christmas. I love everything about the season. Okay, maybe I don't love the traffic jams surrounding the perimeter of the mall for my last-minute shopping, but I really don't mind the jostling crowds once I get inside. The energy and sense of anticipation is palpable and contagious, even when the checkout lines stretch down aisles and outside the store.

I love buying gifts for Amy, my six children, extended family, and friends. I believe that I actually like giving gifts more than getting gifts at Christmas, though I'd be lying if I told you I don't love cutting ribbon and unwrapping shiny and colorful paper to see what I got too.

I love visiting with the friends and neighbors I don't see enough during the year, having my family gather in my home, hosting a couple of parties, putting up and admiring bright and beautiful decorations—or at least assisting Amy with the task of putting them up—and crooning the songs of the season. When not playing one of our countless Christmas CDs, we set the radio in the house on one of those stations that play nothing but Christmas music for a month. I don't care if the kids think I'm just a little bit silly as I sing along with Bing Crosby, Nat King Cole, and Perry Como.

I love how Christmas allows me to feel childlike delight. There are more wonders within the season than there is space for me to list them here, though the following pages make a small attempt at that. But I must add that what I love most about Christmas is the Christmas story itself. Not just the beautiful words to the poignant drama, but the spiritual truth, the divine event behind them.

Years ago, my heart and mind were captured with the reality that God loves us all so much—that God loves me so much—that He sent a Baby to bring light to a dark world. Isn't it amazing what can happen in one's life through the power of a simple story? And is it any wonder I feel so blessed each day and that I've spent my adult life trying to be an encouragement and blessing to others?

This season, maybe as you read this book as a daily Advent devotional or something you read aloud with your family, I hope you experience the simple blessings of Christmas in your heart and life. And that what you experience you'll share with those you love and everyone who is around you.

Merry Christmas!
Mark Gilroy

1

Christmas
Teaches Us That
Greatness Begins
in Small Packages

It comes every year and will go on forever.
And along with Christmas belong the keepsakes
and the customs. Those humble, everyday things
a mother clings to, and ponders, like Mary
in the secret spaces of her heart.

MARJORIE HOLMES

The kingdom of heaven is like a mustard seed, which a man took
and planted in his field. Though it is the smallest of all seeds, yet
when it grows, it is the largest of garden plants and becomes a
tree, so that the birds come and perch in its branches.

MATTHEW 13:31–32

The man who is called "father" by three of the world's major religions—Islam, Christianity, and Judaism—had but a small family of his own. In fact, he and his wife, Sarah, weren't sure they could even have one child. But from Abraham's offspring, there remains a lineage that circles the globe.

He wasn't supposed to live beyond infancy. All the other baby boys of his birthplace died the year he was born. His mother had to give him up to the care of another. But the tiny baby survived, even when he was floated down the Nile River in a basket. The man Moses grew into led his people out of slavery and, against impossible circumstances presented by nature and enemies, he brought them into God's Promised Land.

He was the youngest son of an inconsequential family that was a member of a small tribe that lived in the hill country of an obscure nation. Yet David, a man after God's own heart, prevailed in combat against lion, bear, and giant. Poet and warrior, he became a king and nation builder against whom all other kings to come would be measured.

In a dark and violent world, in a bleak and blighted village, a tiny life appeared. What difference does the life of one small baby make? Particularly one of questionable lineage, of humble means, far from the center of worldly power?

Jesus, the Babe in the manger, brought light and hope to a world engulfed in strife—and forever changed the course of history.

We look to the big, expensive, and impressive; we admire the powerful and influential; we check price tags, even during the holidays. But the message of Christmas is that great things come in small packages. A simple kindness. A gentle word. A smile. A listening ear. A shared meal. A song. A handwritten note. A surprise phone call. The shining eyes of children.

All these small gestures hint at the greatest blessing of Christmas: a grand and magnificent love broke into the world when Jesus was born in a humble manger.

Enjoy the bright lights and big moments of the season. But don't lose sight of the fact that the greatest blessings come in the smallest packages.

2

Christmas
Helps Us Reconnect
with Scattered
Friends and Family

Christmas—that magic blanket that wraps itself about us,
that something so intangible that it is like a fragrance.
It may weave a spell of nostalgia. Christmas may be
a day of feasting, or of prayer, but always it will be
a day of remembrance—a day in which we think
of everything we have ever loved.

AUGUSTA E. RUNDEL

And over all these virtues put on love,
which binds them all together in perfect unity.

COLOSSIANS 3:14

The greeting card industry has been around a lot longer than Hallmark Cards, American Greetings, Recycled Paper Greetings, and other social expression companies.

Ancient Chinese and Egyptian civilizations had a tradition among the wealthy of sending simple prepackaged blessings and well wishes to loved ones on papyrus or clay surfaces. It was in fifteenth-century Europe that handmade and commissioned greeting cards became a common expression of affection and love. And yes, these simple and lavish handcrafts were often sent during the holidays, especially Valentine's Day and Christmas. In America, the greeting card industry blossomed in the middle of the nineteenth century as commercial printing boomed and with the advent of the postage stamp. During the Victorian Era, Christmas and greeting cards became entwined.

For two centuries, Christmas has been a time to update mailing lists and send friends and family lovely cards that include a little bit of news and well wishes—and, of course, to eagerly check the mailbox each day to see who has sent a card to you.

Now, our mailing lists might be electronic or found only in our social networks. In addition to paper and ink and foils, the cards we receive might be found on a friend's blog site or arrive in our inbox as e-cards or lavishly designed family newsletters.

But the purpose is the same. Christmas reminds us to catch up with the people who have come and gone in our lives but for whom we still feel love, affection, and attachment. Our Christmas correspondence, no matter what form it takes, also stands as a living history of our lives. Those mailing lists and colorful cards show us the phases we've lived through, the joys and sorrows, the events and memories of how we got to where we are now, the people who are special and have meant so much to us.

Christmas reminds us that staying connected, even when our relationships are scattered, may be a challenge, but it is also a blessing that is more than worth the effort.

3

Christmas Reveals the Wisdom of Childlike Wonder

Christmas! The very word brings joy to our hearts.
No matter how we may dread the rush,
the long Christmas lists for gifts and cards
to be bought and given—when Christmas Day comes
there is still the same warm feeling we had as children,
the same warmth that enfolds our hearts and our homes.

JOAN WINMILL BROWN

[Jesus] called a little child to him, and placed the child among
them. And he said: "Truly I tell you, unless you change and
become like little children, you will never enter the kingdom of
heaven. Therefore, whoever takes the lowly position of this child
is the greatest in the kingdom of heaven."

MATTHEW 18:2–4

Even though little Cindy Lou Who didn't stop the Grinch from stealing Christmas, most Dr. Seuss experts still think it was her big blue eyes that first pierced his heart and began his personal transformation, even before he heard the whole community singing from his icy hilltop home.

What are the characteristics of a grinch?

Nothing showcases the heart of a grinch better than cynicism: looking at everyone and everything with jaded and jaundiced eyes. A true grinch would never be satisfied with watching another person perform a good deed during the holidays, but would take time to wonder who that person is trying to impress.

Isolation is another surefire way of showing the world your inner grinch. Getting together with family and friends can be too much of a hassle, can't it? Why go to a special church service when you've had enough of crowds at the mall? And the neighborhood progressive dinner will conflict with a TV show you wanted to watch!

Then there's a resentful spirit that hates to see others experiencing blessings in life. Such a small-spirited outlook declares one to be a top-tier grinch.

But there's more that goes into being a grinch. Irritability. Short temper. Meanness. Making fun of others for their innocence and joy.

Now if you've had enough of being a grinch, there is a cure if you've seriously been feeling like canceling Christmas for yourself—and everyone else—this year. It begins with humility or not believing you are too sophisticated and cultured to stop and admire the tinsel and the toys. It continues with the words of Jesus to His followers when some thought the children were being a nuisance and distracting them from grown-up concerns. He said, "Let the little children come to me, and do not hinder them, for the kingdom of heaven belongs to such as these" (Matthew 19:14).

Lost the wonder of Christmas? Maybe you need to watch a child enjoying the season. Whatever it takes, spend some time with children this Christmas. Have some friends or family members with children come over to decorate cookies. Take a family you know on a Christmas light tour or to an outdoor nativity scene. Or help an organization that delivers toys to needy children, and see if you can be part of the delivery team.

Children approach Christmas activities with unabashed enthusiasm. Watching their excitement and outright glee over things as simple as sugar cookies and wrapping paper, you just might find your heart softening—or growing three sizes—and your cynicism melting. You'll be filled with compassion for children and an appreciation for their ability to really celebrate. Best of all, your hard heart will be replaced with a renewed sense of childlike wonder and joy.

4

Christmas
Reminds Us That
Generosity Brings
Joy to Others—
and Ourselves

The joy of brightening other lives, bearing others' burdens, easing others' loads and supplanting empty hearts and lives with generous gifts becomes for us the magic of Christmas.

W. C. JONES

The Lord Jesus himself said:
"It is more blessed to give than to receive."

ACTS 20:35

Jim and Della Young. A young couple just starting out in the world together and living in a hardscrabble furnished tenement in New York City that cost eight dollars per week. Sure, they were poor, but they were in love, so all was well—until the Christmas season rolled around.

Through shrewd bargaining with grocers and other shopkeepers, Della had managed to save money to buy a Christmas gift for Jim. Her problem was that she couldn't buy much with $1.87. She was beside herself with tears.

Jim had fared little better. But when he arrived home from work on Christmas Eve, he carefully carried a treasure he knew Della would adore, all wrapped in tissue and paper and tied with a string.

But the only thing on Della's mind was a gift she had for Jim. She could barely contain her excitement in anticipation of seeing the expression of joy on his face when he opened what she had found for him.

Della's pride was her hair: "rippling and shining like a cascade of brown waters. It reached below her knee and made itself almost a garment for her." Jim's pride was a gold watch that had been owned by his father and grandfather.

Jim's gift to her was a set of combs, "side and back, that Della had worshipped long in a Broadway window. Beautiful combs, pure tortoise shell, with jeweled rims."

Della's gift to Jim was a "platinum fob chain simple and chaste in design, properly proclaiming its value by substance alone and not by meretricious ornamentation—as all good things should do. It was even worthy of The Watch."

All was wonderful except the small detail that Jim had sold his watch to buy Della's combs—and Della had sold her hair to a wigmaker in order to buy his chain.

But in his classic short story, "The Gift of the Magi," William Sydney Porter, better known to the world as O. Henry, wrote:

> *The magi, as you know, were wise men—wonderfully wise men—who brought gifts to the Babe in the manger. They invented the art of giving Christmas presents. Being wise, their gifts were no doubt wise ones, possibly bearing the privilege of exchange in case of duplication. And here I have lamely related to you the uneventful chronicle of two foolish children in a flat who most unwisely sacrificed for each other the greatest treasures of their house. But in a last word to the wise of these days let it be said that of all who give gifts these two were the wisest. Of all who give and receive gifts, such as they are wisest. Everywhere they are wisest. They are the magi.*

The Christmas season is fun and exciting as we open presents, but it is even more joyful for the opportunity to share from our abundance with others.

5

Christmas Calls Us to Peace with All People— Even Those Different from Ourselves

Christmas is not a time or a season,
but a state of mind. To cherish peace
and goodwill, to be plenteous in mercy,
is to have the real spirit of Christmas.

CALVIN COOLIDGE

Glory to God in the highest heaven,
and on earth peace to those on whom his favor rests.

LUKE 2:14

It happened amid the fiercest fighting of World War I. It spanned all five hundred miles of the western front, a jagged, ever-changing line separating British and German forces. Newspapers around the world hailed it as a miracle.

There are numerous firsthand accounts from soldiers' journals of how this seemingly spontaneous outburst got started. But the story most remembered was that a German soldier began singing "Stille Nacht," and his solo soon became a chorus as he was joined by English voices singing "Silent Night." A British regiment serenaded the Germans with "The First Noel," and the Germans sang back to them, "O Tannenbaum."

Men from both armies laid down their weapons and crept cautiously and then quickly into no-man's-land to share food, cigars, and drinks, and even play a game of soccer together.

Christmas has always been a time when people of all ages, races, and creeds come together to break bread peacefully. As in the Christmas Truce of 1914, sometimes even sworn enemies have laid aside historical and more recent hostilities.

In the Christmas story, a newborn Baby was given gifts by wise men from the East, probably Persians from a city in what is now Iran. When these Magi realized that King Herod was a threat to the Baby's life, they protected him by returning home by a different route to keep his location a secret from the madman. This Baby was sheltered during his childhood in Egypt, a country that had fought many wars with his homeland.

When angels sang to shepherds, "Peace on Earth, goodwill to all men," they announced the simple yet profound truth that enemies can be reconciled, that strangers can become friends, that those who think and believe differently can still be neighbors. Christmas was literally born in strife, but celebrated and protected by "foreigners" who were men and women of peace and goodwill.

As you experience the Christmas season this year, don't think that peace is something to be negotiated by politicians between lands and peoples that are thousands of miles from your world. Begin with how you look at those who are different from you. Does your attitude proclaim that you are a person of peace and goodwill? Move closer to home and ask yourself if you have a relationship where you need to lay down weapons of anger and harmful words. Is there a person with whom you need to call a truce and be reconciled, not just for a day but from this point forward?

6

Christmas Declares That Hardships Don't Last

The spirit of Christmas can be so wonderfully wrapped up in our hearts, and our way of life, that it is readily manifested by our love and prayers; thus can we make more certain peace on earth to men of good will.

GEORGE R. ILES

Weeping may stay for the night,
but rejoicing comes in the morning.

PSALM 30:5

Mary. A peasant girl. Pregnant but unmarried. Subject by law and custom to stoning or, at minimum, a lifetime of shame. It doesn't get much harder than that.

Joseph. A respected leader in his community. Engaged to be married to a young woman he adored. His life turned upside down by a seeming betrayal and the whispers that he had been cheated on. It doesn't hurt much deeper than that.

A young couple. Just getting started in an already shaky marriage. She pregnant. Both living under a repressive political regime. Forced to travel at the very time when she most needed rest and warmth. An arduous journey by foot and atop a bumpy, swaying, stumbling donkey. Hard indeed.

They arrived at their destination. Finally. But there were no accommodations available. Couldn't they get a break?

Life can get bumpy for all of us. Just when we think we've arrived, we see the "no occupancy" sign lit brightly. Maybe our road is not as long and as difficult as this couple's, but all of us have experienced the hurts and bruises of life.

For some, life gets even harder around Christmas. It is a reminder of mistakes, lost opportunities, and broken relationships.

Yet even before that first Christmas so long ago, Mary exclaimed, "My soul glorifies the Lord and my spirit rejoices in God my Savior, for he has been mindful of the humble state of his servant" (Luke 1:46–48). Mary knew that even when the road ahead looks stormy, and even when rain and gales storm overhead, we can rest and rejoice in the knowledge that God sees us. He knows where we are. He knows what we need.

Just when the young couple thinks their backs might break, that they'll never find a place to drop their burdens, a soft, warm, dry space is found. There is rest. And a Baby is born. Shepherds and wise men gather. Angels sing. Stars shine brighter than ever before.

Christmas reminds us that hardship doesn't last. God smiles on mother and child—and on us.

7

Christmas Calls for a Celebration

Perhaps the best Yuletide decoration
is being wreathed in smiles.

UNKNOWN

Rejoice in the Lord always.
I will say it again: Rejoice!

PHILIPPIANS 4:4

There is a rhythm to life that includes work, rest, worship, and play. God has planted the need for all four of these movements in the song that is your life, even if some serious-minded friends might scoff at the notion that play is ordained by God. Play is built around activities that are light, fun, and spontaneous, and that just doesn't seem serious and sober enough for some. Certainly not religious.

Another word for play is *recreation*. And that's just what happens when we play: we are re-created, receiving new energy and enthusiasm for our work and worship.

It's true that in life we are called to exhibit self-control, soberness, discipline, and thoughtful consideration, but there is also a time to celebrate, to let loose, and to simply have a party.

Christmas is most definitely a time for serious reflection and worship. But don't let anyone steal from your life the joy of celebration that is part of the Christmas season.

Maybe some revelers went too far in the Middle Ages. Some medieval celebrations involved imbibing too much and engaging in revelry that crossed the line into debauchery. But is it possible that the Puritans were just as wrong? They banned Christmas in an effort to purge the church of decadence. They even banned going to mass and things as innocent as mince pies.

Jesus, the Author of Christmas, the One we worship and celebrate at Christmas, was criticized sharply for attending parties: "The Son of Man came eating and drinking, and they say, 'Here is a glutton and a drunkard, a friend of tax collectors and sinners.' But wisdom is proved right by her deeds" (Matthew 11:19).

One of Jesus's most famous stories was of a son who wandered far from home, squandering all the material and moral resources his father had given him. But when the son did finally come to his senses and return to his family, his father's immediate response was to throw a huge party to celebrate having his son back home.

Christmas is a time when many return home for the holidays—in both a literal and a figurative sense. Will you be having the time of your life at the party the father has thrown for his lost son or standing aside in judgment with the older son?

When we truly come home for Christmas, we rediscover that our Heavenly Father loves us so much, He gave the gift of His Son.

That calls for a celebration!

8

Christmas
Teaches Gratitude

Christmas day is a day of joy and charity.
May God make you very rich in both.

PHILLIPS BROOKS

Every good and perfect gift is from above,
coming down from the Father of the heavenly lights,
who does not change like shifting shadows.

JAMES 1:17

There is a simple attitude that helps us determine whether we are rich or poor, blessed or cursed, and fundamentally positive or negative about life. To make that enormous of a difference, that attitude must be incredibly powerful. And it is. That attitude is gratitude.

One person gets a job and is thrilled to be a contributing member of a team—and to be paid for it to boot. Another person gets the same job with the same company, with the same pay and benefits, and feels cheated. One person has a great job, and the other has an equally crummy job. Why? The difference is an attitude of gratitude.

One teen looks under the Christmas tree, finds a simple and thoughtful gift from her mom, and knows she is loved; all that another teen can think about as he tears the glossy wrapping paper from the box is the new smartphone he didn't get. She had a great Christmas morning and got absolutely everything she wanted; he had a lousy Christmas and didn't get anything good. Again, the only difference is gratitude.

After a long pregnancy that generated more questions than congratulations, that nearly ended a marriage before it started, that included a painful and arduous journey, that culminated in her son being born in conditions fit for animals but not for humans, how did Mary respond? Luke tells us that she "treasured up all these things and pondered them in her heart" (2:19). In Bethlehem, among the animals, she found joy.

She could have complained that God was doing nothing good for her, that her husband was a lousy provider, that the innkeeper should be put in prison for denying her a bed in the inn, but instead, she declared the "great things" God had done (Luke 1:49).

This central Christmas story—and the joys and challenges of our modern holiday—remind us that gratitude changes everything. Whether there are gifts stacked to the ceiling with your name on them or you aren't sure anyone is going to give you anything, stop and give thanks to God, the giver of all good and perfect gifts.

You'll receive a special blessing in your spirit and discover you have everything you need.

9

Christmas Shows
the Power of Laughter

Fail not to call to mind, in the course of the twenty-fifth of this month, that the Divinest Heart that ever walked the earth was born on that day; and then smile and enjoy yourselves for the rest of it; for mirth is also of Heaven's making.

LEIGH HUNT

A cheerful heart is good medicine.

PROVERBS 17:22

It seems that a new one comes out every year. Nearly every Thanksgiving weekend, theaters release a new Christmas movie—or three! Many of them land in cinematic obscurity shortly after New Year's Day and are only mentioned in trivia games. Others, like 1983's *A Christmas Story* or 1990's *Home Alone*, become insta-classics and run seemingly nonstop on cable channels throughout December for years to come. Tellingly, most Christmas movies are not dark dramas but family-friendly comedies. Christmas movies fill an important niche of holiday entertainment enjoyed by families spending time together. After all, at Christmastime, people want to laugh and have fun.

A night of board games with all the family in town. Laughing out loud at memories of Christmases past. Giggling and mugging for selfies while frosting sugar cookies. Some of the best moments of Christmas are moments of laughter, and laughter is good for the soul and body alike.

Many medical researchers believe that laughter supports the immune system and increases oxygen flow to the muscles. And we all know that a good laugh can lighten even the heaviest of spiritual loads.

Of course, the Christmas season is a time for reflection. It's a time for worship and giving to others and counting our blessings. But it's also a time to celebrate. Besides, counting our blessings has a way of making us feel content, and when we're content, we're free to let loose with laughter.

Enjoy a few laughs this Christmas season. Look for opportunities to share laughter with others, and you'll be enjoying one of the best blessings of the Christmas season.

So I commend the enjoyment of life, because there is nothing better for a person under the sun than to eat and drink and be glad. Then joy will accompany them in their toil all the days of the life God has given them under the sun.

ECCLESIASTES 8:15

10

Christmas
Helps Us See
That Angels
Watch Over Us

Believers, look up—take courage.
The angels are nearer than you think.

BILLY GRAHAM

Praise the Lord, you his angels,
you mighty ones who do his bidding, who obey his word.

PSALM 103:20

Angels play a leading role in the story of Jesus's birth. They appear to Joseph in a dream and tell him of the coming child. The angel Gabriel appears to Mary to tell her she has been chosen by God. And then a heavenly choir proclaims the message of the Christ child to the shepherds.

But we have to wonder if angels played a behind-the-scenes role in the events of Jesus's birth as well. Mary and Joseph's journey to Bethlehem would have been difficult and dangerous. Doesn't it make sense to think that angels helped them find their way and arrive at just the right time? Mary gave birth—her first birth—in a barn full of animals with no midwives, no modern or ancient medicine, and no place to put the baby other than the manger. Under those circumstances, it seems that Providence was watching out for the young family—through the care of angels, perhaps?

Psalm 91 declares, "For he will command his angels concerning you to guard you in all your ways; they will lift you up in their hands, so that you will not strike your foot against a stone" (verses 11–12). Angels showed up in Bible stories to deliver big messages directly from God. But the Bible also seems to indicate that God sends them to surround us and watch over us, that they're there all the time. Christmas, with its little everyday miracles and blessings, has a special way of comforting us with reminders of the presence of angels.

Sometime this Christmas, you're bound to find yourself in the presence of a Christmas tree—maybe even your own—with a glowing angel beaming down at you, a peaceful smile on her face and a halo on her head. Okay, it's true, all angels in the Bible are male, and the angel on your tree is fashioned more for decoration than to communicate spiritual truth. But you know that profound truths often hide behind imperfect representations. Let the angel atop your tree be a reminder that God watches over you and that His angels stand beside you.

See, I am sending an angel ahead of you to guard you along the way and to bring you to the place I have prepared.

EXODUS 23:20

11

Christmas Inspires Us with Beauty

Christmas hath a beauty lovelier
than the world can show.

CHRISTINA ROSSETTI

He has made everything beautiful in its time.
He has also set eternity in the human heart; yet no one
can fathom what God has done from beginning to end.

ECCLESIASTES 3:11

In 2011, Americans spent $6 billion on Christmas decorations. It's not hard to see where that kind of money goes. Many of our streets turn into winter wonderlands each December, with lights twinkling, reindeer flying, and Santa dancing. Of course, some decoration schemes are more tasteful than others. And while some garish displays might earn grimaces from passersby, others make us stop in our tracks and take in the view. Pale, twinkling lights gracing the eaves and a bright red ribbon adorning the door are beautiful sights.

Bible scholar N. T. Wright says that our appreciation for beauty is one of the things that indicates our need for God—that our longing for beautiful things represents a longing for another world and the presence of God. Perhaps that longing intensifies at Christmastime, because we fill our homes with beautiful things.

The elements of the Christmas story have inspired art for ages. The Madonna-and-child theme has been rendered in all types of media by countless artists, including Michelangelo, da Vinci, Caravaggio, Rubens, and Salvador Dalí. The nativity scene can also be found in many iterations throughout art history. There's something about Christmas that inspires beauty—striking, colorful images as well as music and literature that seem nothing short of divinely inspired. And beauty in turn inspires us. It stirs something inside us, causes us to pause and perhaps pray. Beauty can be a powerful motivator and enriches our lives.

This Christmas, slow down long enough to enjoy something beautiful. Let it fill your heart with joy and wonder at the inexpressible truths of Christmas. And let it make your Christmas season truly blessed.

When I consider your heavens, the work of your fingers,
the moon and the stars, which you have set in place,
what is mankind that you are mindful of them,
human beings that you care for them?

PSALM 8:3–4

12

Christmas Encourages
Us to Open Our Hearts
and Homes to Others

Christmas is the season for kindling the fire
of hospitality in the hall, the genial flame
of charity in the heart.

WASHINGTON IRVING

Do not forget to show hospitality to strangers,
for by so doing some people have shown hospitality
to angels without knowing it.

HEBREWS 13:2

History and literature brim with accounts of the wonderful gift of hospitality. In Charles Dickens's immortal and beloved *A Christmas Carol*, it is the rich man with the big house, Ebenezer Scrooge, who locks his door and heart tightly to others, content to count his solid gold and silver coins. It takes an ethereal ghost and the fear of what the afterlife—chains and all—might hold for him to awaken Scrooge to the dour and cruel miserliness of his ways. Soon after he sees the light, he is welcomed into the humble home of Bob Cratchit, where the air is cold but the hearts are warm, where he sees with his own eyes the responsibility and richness of opening one's heart and home to others.

You might be thinking, *but my house isn't very big and my furniture isn't very nice*. We get so tired out by the holidays. We just want some downtime.

Not sure about your gift of hospitality? First of all, if you have a smile, a warm heart, and a few kind words, no one cares about how grand or simple your house is. Motivational speaker Zig Ziglar said, "Money will buy you a bed, but not a good night's sleep, a house, but not a home, a companion, but not a friend."

Second, you are wise to pace yourself over the Christmas season and not fill every square in your December calendar with activities. You need not feel guilty for that downtime you've been looking forward to.

But the simple truth is that hospitality is good for the soul; it allows you to connect with others and is a tangible expression of your care for them.

Two thousand years ago, an unnamed innkeeper, his guest rooms already filled, opened his heart and what accommodations he could muster to a young couple with nowhere else to turn. His home was the site of the greatest miracle in the history of mankind.

Shepherds and angels may not appear at your front door when you invite the neighbors over, but a special blessing awaits you and them!

13

Christmas Teaches
the Importance
of Simple Acts
of Kindness

*Blessed is the season which engages
the whole world in a conspiracy of love.*

HAMILTON WRIGHT MABIE

Therefore, as God's chosen people, holy and dearly loved,
clothe yourselves with compassion, kindness,
humility, gentleness and patience.

COLOSSIANS 3:12

Norman Vincent Peale, noted minister and author from the previous century, tells the story of a young girl from Sweden spending Christmas in big, bustling New York City. She was living with an American family and helping them around the house, and she didn't have much money. So she knew she couldn't get them a very nice Christmas present. Besides, they already had so much, with new gifts arriving every day.

With just a little money in her pocket, she went out and bought an outfit for a small baby, and then she set out on a journey to find the poorest part of town and the poorest baby she could find. At first, she received only strange looks from passersby when she asked them for help. But then a kind stranger, a Salvation Army bell ringer, guided her to a poor part of town and helped her deliver her gift. On Christmas morning, instead of giving them a wrapped present, she told the family she served what she had done in their name. Everyone was speechless, and everyone was blessed—the girl for giving, the wealthy family for seeing others with new eyes, and the poor family for receiving an unexpected gift.

All of us have opportunities both large and small to show kindness, especially at Christmastime. We can help strangers by delivering gifts to needy kids or serving homeless families at a soup kitchen. Or we can simply look for everyday ways to be kind, like allowing someone to go ahead of us in a lengthy line at the department store or giving that bell ringer a little change and a few encouraging words.

Maybe it's because we're in gift-giving mode anyway that giving to others becomes so important at Christmas. Maybe it's because we're more aware of our families and friends and communities. Or maybe it's because two thousand years ago, the earth received the most perfect, most loving gift of all, helping us to understand true kindness.

Whatever the reason, don't let Christmas pass you by without showing kindness to someone. Because it is truly more blessed to give than to receive.

14

Christmas
Challenges Us to
Make Our Lives Matter

Many people have a wrong idea of what constitutes true happiness. It is not attained through self-gratification, but through fidelity to a worthy purpose.

HELEN KELLER

But I have raised you up for this very purpose, that I might show you my power and that my name might be proclaimed in all the earth.

EXODUS 9:16

After Jesus's birth, Mary and Joseph took Him to the temple to present Him to God and offer a sacrifice, according to their custom. While they were there, an old man named Simeon took the baby and began to praise God, thanking Him for His salvation. God had revealed to Simeon that he would not die before the Messiah came. And when Simeon saw Jesus, he knew that day had come, and he proclaimed the coming Messiah and offered a blessing to Mary and Joseph.

This moment must have stood out in the young parents' minds as another confirmation of who their child really was. It would seem that God had placed Simeon in the right place at the right time.

Each member of the cast of characters in the first Christmas story played a unique role, and each of them furthered God's plan in a way that only he or she could. God needed someone to bring His Son into the world; He chose Mary. Mary needed a protector and provider; God gave her Joseph. The wise men brought gifts and adoration, and the shepherds spread the good news of the baby's birth. God had a plan to enter our world with peace and love, and He used ordinary lives to bring it to fruition.

But the story doesn't end there. God is still working in our world and in our lives, and He invites each of us to fill the role that only we can. At Christmastime, we hear that calling in a unique way. We're moved by the needs around us, and choirs proclaim the good news.

What is God's special purpose for your life? During this Christmas season? Pause. Pray. Listen. Be blessed.

"For I know the plans I have for you," declares the LORD,
*"plans to prosper you and not to harm you,
plans to give you hope and a future."*

JEREMIAH 29:11

15

Christmas Shows
Us That Miracles
Still Happen Today

Whatever else be lost among the years, let us keep Christmas still a shining thing; Whatever doubts assail us, or what fears, let us hold close one day, remembering its poignant meaning for the hearts of men. Let us get back our childlike faith again.

GRACE NOLL CROWELL

I will remember the deeds of the Lord; yes,
I will remember your miracles of long ago.

PSALM 77:11

In her classic book, *Little House on the Prairie*, Laura Ingalls Wilder tells the story of a very special Christmas. Laura and Mary have gone to sleep on Christmas Eve still holding out hope but mostly sad that they won't have a Christmas the next morning because the creek was too high for Santa to cross. Their family friend, Mr. Edwards, wouldn't be able to come either; the weather made even short travel just too dangerous.

But Laura wakes up in the early morning to the sound of their dog growling at someone at the door. It's Mr. Edwards, and he's come all the way to their cabin, crossing the freezing creek with his clothes piled on his head, for Christmas dinner. Best of all, he had met Santa Claus in Independence, Kansas, and the jolly old elf had given him the girls' Christmas presents to deliver since he wouldn't be able to make it to their house himself. There were shiny tin cups and peppermint candy and the most delicate little cakes, along with a shiny new penny for each girl. "It's too much, Edwards," Pa told him. It was a Christmas miracle for which he didn't know how to express his gratitude.

Of course, we know what happened for the Ingalls family was a man-made event, wrought by Mr. Edwards's selflessness and kindness. But does that mean it wasn't a miracle? It certainly was for Laura and Mary. A wonderful blessing of Christmas is that we can expect these kinds of miracles every year. We never know when one will turn up.

There's the miracle of a stranger's kindness to a family down to their last few dollars, the miracle of a surprise card or phone call from an estranged family member, the miracle of cheap seats for a flight home, the miracle of an unexpected Christmas snowfall. The best way to experience

Christmas is with an openness to these little miracles—and a willingness to create miracles for someone else.

Keep your eyes open. Between Thanksgiving and New Year's Eve, anything can happen. Maybe because of something you do.

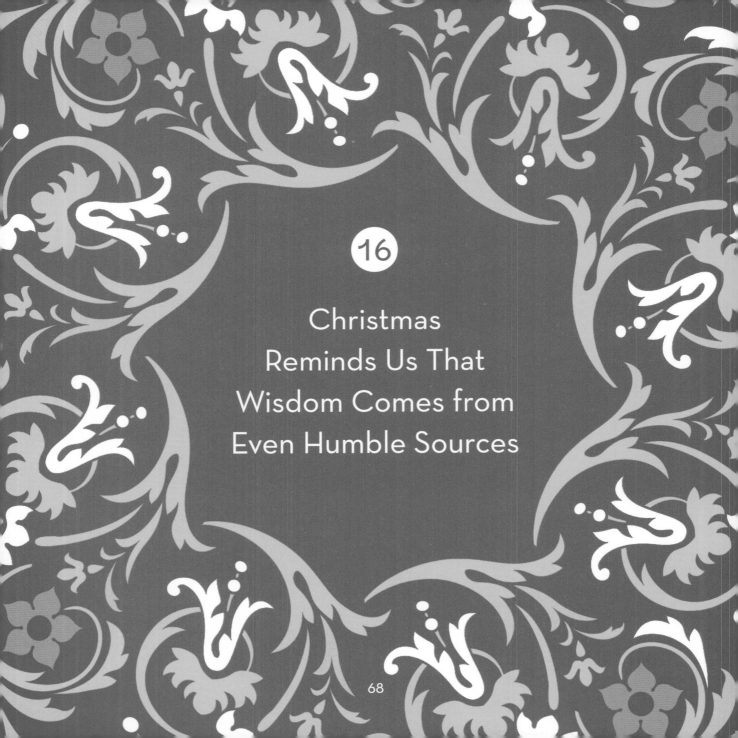

16

Christmas
Reminds Us That
Wisdom Comes from
Even Humble Sources

The Lord of Christmas tide entered into our life
by lowly doors. And still He seeks the lowly doors:
the door of the workshop, the door of the chamber,
and all the unobtrusive doors of human friendship and regard.

J. H. JOWETT

And there were shepherds living out in the fields nearby,
keeping watch over their flocks at night. An angel of the Lord
appeared to them, and the glory of the Lord shone around them.

LUKE 2:8–9

The scene: the temple area. Jesus had overturned the tables of the money changers and begun healing the lame and blind who came to Him. Children began to shout, "Hosanna to the Son of David!" And the high priests and teachers were mad.

They asked Him if He heard the children's voices. In response, He flippantly quoted Psalm 8 and said, "Have you never read, 'From the lips of children and infants you, Lord, have called forth your praise'?" (Matthew 21:14–16).

It wasn't the first time Jesus had encouraged children in their exuberant expression, much to the surprise of those around Him, since children were considered low in social status. Nuisances. Things to be seen but not heard.

On another occasion involving children, the disciples wanted to run off people who brought little children to be blessed by Jesus, only to receive a rebuke from Him in return (Matthew 19:13–15).

Yet another time, Jesus prayed, "I praise you, Father, Lord of heaven and earth, because you have hidden these things from the wise and learned, and revealed them to little children. Yes, Father, for this is what you were pleased to do" (Matthew 11:25–26).

When Jesus Himself was a tiny baby, the news of His birth was announced—by a choir of heavenly angels, no less—not to King Herod but to the shepherds watching their flocks by night. Shepherds too were outcasts of low social status. But those shepherds nonetheless joined the holy family and the wise men in witnessing the birth of the one and only Messiah, and then went on to proclaim the story to all who would listen (Luke 2:8–20). God has a remarkable way of lifting up the lowly, using them to proclaim what really matters most.

So if you're lowly this Christmas—down and out, on the margins, not very influential—take heart: Christmas is for you. The glad tidings of the Baby's birth mean that God is available to you, you have an important place in the Kingdom, and you have something incredibly important to share with others.

And if you're not so lowly—if you're comfortable and on top of your game, if your name carries with it a little bit of weight—Christmas is for you too. It calls you to look and humbly listen for God's message for you today. But to receive this simple blessing of Christmas, you'll have to look and listen closely, because it's quite likely that God will speak to you through the words of a child or another unexpected person you encounter this season.

17

Christmas
Promises Us
New Beginnings

I wake expectant, hoping to see a new thing.

ANNIE DILLARD

Because of the Lord's great love
we are not consumed, for his compassions never fail.
They are new every morning; great is your faithfulness.

LAMENTATIONS 3:22–23

Christmas of 1943 found classically trained dancer Helen Lewis in a work camp. She had been shuffled among camps for two years as the Nazis took power, and she had suffered terribly. In one camp, she and the other detainees were forced to perform backbreaking labor preparing the ground to build an airstrip. Food and water were minimal, and many ill inmates were carted off to the gas chambers. Everyone's spirits were low, and Lewis herself felt as though she might be near death.

But in an odd turn of events, one of the camp guards, who fancied herself an aficionado of culture, decided to organize a camp Christmas show. There would be music, poetry—and dance. Specifically, the ballet *Coppélia*.

Lewis let it slip that she knew the ballet and found herself summoned to assist with the production. And when the other dancers and the camp guard saw her dance abilities, suddenly, things turned brighter for her. She was excused from work to help with the performance. But best of all, as she danced, she said later in Anton Gill's *The Journey Back from Hell*, "I was more alive than I had been in years."

More hardships would follow. But Lewis believed that the extra rest and food—not to mention the chance to do what she loved—preserved her in the face of difficulty and even saved her life.

Christmas is a time to give and a time to stop and think about what really matters. It's also a season of hope. No matter how dark things look, at Christmastime, we're encouraged to think about what's good in the world and anticipate a brighter future. At Christmas, stars glow from the tops of Christmas trees like the star over Bethlehem and fill us with strength to keep going.

Therefore, if anyone is in Christ, the new creation has come: The old has gone, the new is here!

2 CORINTHIANS 5:17

18

Christmas Cautions Us That Not Everyone Is of Goodwill

*Christmas is not just a time for festivity
and merrymaking. It is more than that.
It is a time for the contemplation
of eternal things. The Christmas spirit
is a spirit of giving and forgiving.*

J. C. PENNEY

But test them all; hold on to what is good.

1 THESSALONIANS 5:21

Christmas truly is a time of peace and goodwill toward all people. Herod is a reminder, however, that not all people have goodwill. Just who was this man?

Herod the Great was the son of Antipater, who was politically connected to Julius Caesar but who paid tribute to Caesar's murderers, most notably Brutus. For this, he was poisoned by loyalists to Caesar and the family's political fortunes were suddenly on thin ice. But the young Herod was able to convince Antony and Octavian that his father had been coerced into being disloyal to Julius. In a cunning move, he converted to Judaism and secured the support of both Rome and the Synod of Jerusalem (though the latter support was short-lived). Despite several coup attempts to unseat him, he secured the Herodian dynasty over Jerusalem and Galilee. Along the way, he killed anyone who stood in his path, including his brother, cousins, wife, and even his own mother. He is the madman who was responsible for slaughtering the baby boys of Galilee in an attempt to kill Jesus.

Paranoid and cruel, even on his deathbed, he showed his true colors. He was so worried that no one would mourn his death that he had countless nobles killed so that there would be a general outpouring of grief in the general population to mark his death.

But what does this have to do with Christmas, beyond a cruel footnote on the story of Jesus's birth?

Herod's story offers us a profound lesson: In the midst of joy and peace and comfort, we are reminded that in establishing goodness and mercy, there will be opposition that calls for us to act with courage and wisdom. We shouldn't shy away from doing so. We also shouldn't forget that the Christmas story ultimately ends with Jesus on the cross—and rising again in victory. As hateful and cruel as evil is, good can and will overcome it.

Jesus cautioned his disciples to be as wise as serpents and as innocent as doves. We should be keenly aware of the threats and opposition before us, but we shouldn't let that knowledge steal our comfort and joy.

Is there something you must stand up for—or someone you must stand up to—even in the midst of this Christmas season?

19

Christmas
Shows That God
Is Still at Work
in the World—
and in Our Lives

I heard the bells on Christmas Day

Their old familiar carols play,

And wild and sweet

The words repeat

Of peace on earth, good-will to men!

HENRY WADSWORTH LONGFELLOW

He will be called Wonderful Counselor,
Mighty God, Everlasting Father,
Prince of Peace.

ISAIAH 9:6

In 1863, Charles Longfellow enlisted in the Union Army. By autumn, he had seen plenty of action in battle and endured his share of wartime hardships, including a bout with typhoid fever and malaria. But in late November, he encountered something more critical: a bullet that entered his left shoulder and very nearly left him paralyzed. He was taken home to recover.

"Home" was with his younger brother, Ernest—and his father, Henry Wadsworth Longfellow.

The famous poet was already saddened to the point of depression by the loss of his wife in a tragic accident a short time before the onset of the divisive and bloody Civil War. His son's life-threatening injury only made matters worse and darkened his spirits.

But as he nursed his son back to health that Christmas season, something began to happen in Longfellow's heart. He gave thanks every day that Charles had not been killed in battle, and his heart began to lighten and soften. Out of this experience, he wrote the classic poem, "Christmas Bells," which was set to music and became a beloved Christmas carol called "I Heard the Bells on Christmas Day." The next-to-last few stanzas of Longfellow's original poem bemoan the tragedies and losses of our weary world. But the last verse declares a renewal of hope:

> Then pealed the bells more loud and deep;
> "God is not dead; nor doth He sleep:
> The Wrong shall fail,
> The Right prevail,
> With peace on earth, good-will to men."

The baby in the manger was called Emmanuel—"God with us." When God entered our world that fateful night, He assured us that He was with us and was working out a plan for our healing and hope. Because of this amazing gift, no matter what tragedies we witness or endure, we can rest assured that "God is not dead; nor doth He sleep."

20

Christmas
Reminds Us to
Pause and Reenergize

*I do come home at Christmas. We all do,
or we all should. We all come home, or ought
to come home, for a short holiday—the longer,
the better—from the great boarding school where
we are forever working at our arithmetical slates,
to take, and give a rest.*

CHARLES DICKENS

There remains, then, a Sabbath-rest for the people of God;
for anyone who enters God's rest also rests from their works,
just as God did from his.

HEBREWS 4:9–10

Bob wondered if things could get any worse. Only a few weeks before Christmas, his employer began requiring employees to take rotating unpaid days off due to budget troubles. But he knew he couldn't grumble too hard. After all, at least he still had a job.

His first day off fell on the kids' first day of winter vacation. At first, he greeted the day grumpily. But then, somehow, their excitement got to him. The three of them streamed old Christmas specials, fixed lunch, and finished their Christmas lists (modest ones this year, but still fun to write). Bob realized that the last month or so at work had been fraught with stress as the company struggled and that even though the downtime made him anxious, reconnecting with his kids somehow helped. It helped him reprioritize, and it gave him time to think about his next career moves. He returned to work the next day determined to enjoy the Christmas season and a shade more optimistic about the future.

Maybe it's because Christmas brings a few days off work (for most of us) and out of our routine or because it falls just before the new year, a time for dreaming and planning about the future. Or maybe it's because something about Christmas encourages us to count our blessings and reminds us of things that are truly good and important, like giving to others and living a life of love. Whatever the reason, Christmas is a much-needed opportunity to pause.

The Jewish concept of Sabbath is about more than just not working one day a week. The purpose of Sabbath is to rest, to commemorate how God rested after creation. But it's also about anticipating a different era in time, the Messianic age. In observing a day of rest, we pause from the concerns and stresses of our time and embrace God's time.

Whether your holiday season is slow or packed with activities, Christmas is a different kind of time. And it can be a wonderful one.

If you typically chafe under the forced break from responsibilities that Christmas brings, this year, don't fight it. Pause. Slow down. Take strength from this time of rest, and take stock of where your life is going. The chance to reenergize and be still enough to hear God's voice is one of the most precious gifts of Christmas.

21

Christmas
Calls for Us to Forgive
and Seek Forgiveness

Peace on earth will come to stay,
When we live Christmas every day.

HELEN STEINER RICE

Be kind and compassionate to one another, forgiving each other,
just as in Christ God forgave you.

EPHESIANS 4:32

It had been years since the two brothers had spoken. There had been an argument; harsh words had been exchanged. They left each other alone for some time to cool off, and then they were both too proud to make the first move of reconciliation. Sometimes, they rehearsed the other's wrongs in their minds. Other times, they felt a stirring fondness for each other and a prick of remorse that almost moved their fingers toward the phone—but never quite did.

One Christmas passed. And then another. And one more. With the arrival of each holiday, memories of their childhood together were reanimated. But still, they could not pick up the phone.

It was a son and nephew who unwittingly broke the silence between the brothers. He was eight years old and hadn't seen his uncle and cousins for a while, and as Thanksgiving leftovers chilled in the fridge and discussion turned to plans for Christmas, he asked, "Where are Uncle John and Aunt Kathy? Why don't we see them anymore?"

His dad had no real answer. And as he thought about how much he would hate to be torn apart from his son, he knew he no longer wanted to be torn apart from his brother. He wanted to be able to share his old memories of his brother, and he wanted to make new ones that included his son.

So he picked up the phone.

The conversation was icy and stiff, even a little formal. But the phone call was not unwelcome. And then there was another. And another on Christmas Day. During that one, "I'm sorry for…" was spoken on both ends of the line, quietly, without fanfare or tears. But each "I'm sorry" was heartfelt, and each established forgiveness and a lasting reconciliation.

The next Christmas saw two families celebrating the holiday together again.

Christmas is timeless and spurs us to think about eternal things. It's also a time to reconnect with family and friends. For those two reasons, forgiveness is often the most important part of a meaningful Christmas. Yes, relationships can be difficult. But if Christmas teaches us anything, it's the power of love and sacrificial giving, expressed beautifully in the miracle of forgiveness.

22

Christmas Reminds Us We Are Never Alone

I am not alone at all, I thought. I was never alone at all. And that, of course, is the message of Christmas. We are never alone. Not when the night is darkest, the wind coldest, the world seemingly most indifferent. For this is still the time God chooses.

TAYLOR CALDWELL

The virgin will conceive and give birth
to a son, and they will call him Immanuel
(which means "God with us").

MATTHEW 1:23

It is possible to walk down Fifth Avenue in New York City with a mob of shoppers and window watchers on a Saturday afternoon during the Christmas season, to attend a packed church service to experience Handel's *Messiah*, to stand in a long line at the local movie theater on the opening night of the latest holiday blockbuster everyone has been waiting to see, even to attend the neighborhood Christmas progressive dinner with people you know and greet regularly. It is possible to do all these things and still feel lonely.

David Riesman, a Harvard professor and prominent sociologist of the 1950s, described this "modern" phenomenon as being a member of the "lonely crowd."

If you are feeling disconnected, isolated, and alone in the world, well, you're not alone. As easy as it seems to simply reach out to others, in our fast-paced, media-saturated, competitive, busy, self-centered, preoccupied society, really connecting can be an imposing challenge. Is it any wonder that so many people turn to the virtual world of cyberspace for dating, chatting, socializing, and experiencing relationships rather than savoring flesh-and-blood encounters?

You can do Christmas shopping online, but you just can't do Christmas by yourself. So even if you find yourself alone in a crowd at Christmastime, the spirit of the season—the One who came to bring peace to all people, to reconcile God and man, to lift up and redeem people from every walk of life—will touch your heart. Even if you don't know how to reach out to Him or others, He will reach out to you.

What does it take from you? Nothing more than an open heart. Why? You just don't know how, when, where, and with whom you'll realize you are not alone.

Be strong and courageous. Do not be afraid or terrified because of them, for the LORD your God goes with you; he will never leave you nor forsake you.

DEUTERONOMY 3:16

23

Christmas
Kindles the
Spirit of Service

Happiness...consists in giving,
and in serving others.

HENRY DRUMMOND

Whoever wants to become great among you must be your
servant, and whoever wants to be first must be your slave—
just as the Son of Man did not come to be served, but to serve,
and to give his life as a ransom for many.

MATTHEW 20:26-28

In his classic short novel, *Journey to the East*, Herman Hesse recasts the story of the Magi's journey. A band of rich and powerful men have been recruited for an adventure that promises them great wealth and glory. They don't know the name of the mysterious man who put the pilgrimage together; they don't even know the final destination of their journey. Their only information comes through a humble servant, Leo, who prepares their food, polishes their boots, and plays the guitar and sings to them each night as they fall asleep.

The sojourners jockey for position and bicker among themselves about who should be the leader and make decisions, while no one but Leo accepts the mantle of serving the group. One by one, the men desert the party to try and return home, all but broken by this grand failure. With the complete collapse of the expedition, one of the men, bitter and angry, determines that he will find the mysterious sponsor of the scheme to find out what went wrong and give him a piece of his mind.

It takes him years and great effort, but he finally tracks down this shadowy and mysterious character, only to discover that the great patron was Leo all along. In explaining why the expedition failed, Leo pointed out what the man already knew in his heart: great tasks require great servants.

Christmas has a way of calling our attention to those less fortunate in our own neighborhoods, of making us more aware of the needs in our communities, of acquainting us with the joy of giving to others. And while it's true that each one of us is responsible for our own pursuit of happiness, Christmas reminds us of another powerful truth: we're all in this together.

We can influence the direction of our families, churches, and communities. The very first step is taking the role of servant to others. When St. Paul wrote about Jesus coming to earth, he wrote one of the great affirmations of Christendom:

[Jesus], being in very nature God,
did not consider equality with God something to be used to his own advantage;
rather, he made himself nothing
by taking the very nature of a servant,
being made in human likeness.
And being found in appearance as a man,
he humbled himself
by becoming obedient to death—
even death on a cross!

Philippians 2:6–8

This Christmas, experience the blessing of giving sacrificially and serving those around you. Their lives, your own life, and the life you share together may never be the same.

24

Christmas
Reminds Us to
Cherish Memories
of Loved Ones

*Our hearts grow tender with childhood memories
and love of kindred, and we are better throughout
the year for having, in spirit, become a child again
at Christmas-time.*

LAURA INGALLS WILDER

Dear friends, let us love one another,
for love comes from God.

1 JOHN 4:7

I remember the first time my family stayed home for Christmas instead of traveling to Grandma's house in Detroit. I was seven years old. And I knew that it didn't feel right.

At Grandma's house, there was always a real Christmas tree. At our house that year, we had a dinky little silver tree.

At Grandma's house, there were tins filled with "million dollar" fudge. There were cookies and other treats at our house but no "million dollar" fudge.

At Grandma's house, Grandma was there. Not at our house.

At Grandma's house, there were Uncle Ray, Aunt Esther, Aunt Naomi, and Uncle Dale to fawn over me. At our house, it was just my parents, my sisters, and me. We had great fun together. But that year, something was missing.

When Grandma's house was sold, our family began gathering in Washington, DC. But the house wasn't what really mattered. The traditions lived on: a never-ending drive with never-ending songs, a Christmas tree, Monopoly and other board games (that never made us bored), "million dollar" fudge, reading Luke 2 on Christmas morning, and of course, Grandma.

I can't remember another Christmas without Grandma until we started gathering every other year because of extended families. The years without Grandma still didn't seem right. And Christmas has never been quite the same since she died. The last time I saw her was on a Christmas Day. A few weeks later, the family gathered to cry, grieve, celebrate, laugh, and pay last respects.

Christmas is almost necessarily nostalgic. The very arrival of December stirs memories of Christmases past and the traditions we keep to bring them fully to life. That's one reason traditions and family gatherings are so important: they create memories we can relive in the future. Memories can bring us joy and comfort and fill our hearts with gratitude.

But as we remember the past, we should not only recall the fun times we had, but also remember with love the people who created those memories with us. My grandma made my childhood Christmases what they were. And each year, I feel moved not only by the memory of fudge and games and Christmas trees, but by the memory of Grandma herself. I remember her faith and her steadfast love for her family.

This year, as you recall Christmases past, pause to honor the loved ones who live on in your memory, even if it's only with a brief, silent prayer. Remember that you have been blessed with people to love, people who have loved you. And thank God for the blessing of traditions and memories.

25

Christmas
Invites Us to Worship

Come and behold Him, Born the King of Angels.
O come, let us adore Him…Christ the Lord.

JOHN WADE

Know that the Lord is God. It is he who made us, and we are
his; we are his people, the sheep of his pasture… For the Lord
is good and his love endures forever; his faithfulness continues
through all generations.

PSALM 100:3, 5

When Englishman John Wade penned the immortal words to "O Come All Ye Faithful," he beautifully captured a vision of that first Christmas, when mother and father, wise men and shepherds, and even beasts of burden simply "adored" the Baby in a manger.

St. Francis of Assisi is the man credited with creating the first living nativity. The thirteenth-century priest was troubled that the peasants he served had such little understanding of the Christian faith and the central truths of the gospel. So he gathered an ox and a donkey, a manger, and some hay and began to preach on the birth of Jesus. In his biography of St. Francis, St. Bonaventure said that the priest could not even say the baby's name "for the tenderness of His love" and called him the Babe of Bethlehem.

We have a way of making things more complicated than they really are. That's not a new affliction nor reserved as a condition of our modern world. Two thousand years ago, when a group of professors and clergy had a spokesman ask Jesus what was most important in obeying God, He stunned them with his simplicity:

> "The most important one," answered Jesus, "is this: 'Hear, O Israel: the Lord our God, the Lord is one. Love the Lord your God with all your heart and with all your soul and with all your mind and with all your strength.' The second is this: 'Love your neighbor as yourself.' There is no commandment greater than these."
>
> Mark 12:29–31

Can anything be added to what matters most for you today? And can anything be more important for you this Christmas than simple worship?

Worship is different from thanksgiving. Thanksgiving is expressing gratitude for what God has done for us. He has redeemed us and blessed us in countless ways. Worship, on the other hand, looks behind what God has done and expresses awe, reverence, and admiration for those attributes of God that lead Him to treat us with so much favor. His goodness. His mercy. His faithfulness. His power.

Where do you even begin to worship God this Christmas season? It can happen in a church service or the reading of a Scripture passage with your family or in a time of prayer or so many other ways. But maybe this is the year to reach back across the generations and simplify—just as Francis did. Why not find a living nativity in your community and simply stand in wonder as you adore the baby in a manger?

About the Author

Mark Gilroy is a publisher, author, consultant, blogger, positive thinker, believer, encourager, and family guy. A resident of Brentwood, Tennessee, he has six kids, with one in college and five out in the "real world." Mark has had a long, varied, and successful career in publishing, from his first paid creative assignment as a newspaper sports writer while in college, to serving as head of gift, specialty, and backlist publishing for Thomas Nelson, the world's largest Christian publisher. Throughout his journey in the world of books, he has worked with leading authors such as Max Lucado, Sarah Young, John Maxwell, Darlene Zschech, H. Jackson Brown, Donald Miller, Billy Graham, George Foreman, and many others.

All biblical verses are used as reflected in the
New International Version (NIV) of the Christian Bible.

Published by Simple Truths, an imprint of Sourcebooks, Inc.
P.O. Box 4410, Naperville, Illinois 60567-4410
(630) 961-3900
Fax: (630) 961-2168
www.sourcebooks.com

Printed and bound in China.
HH 10 9 8 7 6 5 4 3 2 1

CHANGE STARTS WITH **SOMETHING SIMPLE.**

Pick from hundreds of titles at:
SimpleTruths.com

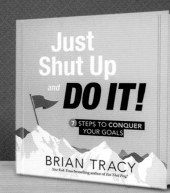

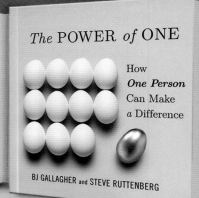

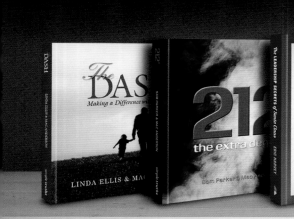

▷ Shop for books on themes like teamwork, success, leadership, customer service, motivation and more.

Call us toll-free at **1-800-900-3427**